Diamond Capsules
for Success and Wisdom

Diamond Capsules
for Success and Wisdom

ARNOLD ZEGARELLI

Published by Zegarelli, Inc.
177 Shadow Ridge Drive
Pittsburgh PA 15238

Library of Congress Catalog Card Number: 98-96202

ISBN 0-9663688-0-0

Book and jacket design by Helen m Worsing

Manufactured in the United States of America

10   9   8   7   6   5   4   3   2   1

To my wife, Dolores, my heart;
my brother, Robert, my soul;
and my children, Ronda and Gregg, my legacy.

ABOUT THE AUTHOR

Arnold Zegarelli is a self-made, successful businessman, a motivational speaker, and an icon in the beauty industry. One of the most dynamic hair styling leaders in the U.S., he is the founder and president of Zegarelli, Inc.; chairman of the board of directors of Arnold Zegarelli Products, Inc.; creative consultant and advisor to the chairman of Premier Salons International, Inc.; and hair styling director of Lazarus Hair Salons in Pittsburgh, Pennsylvania.

Well known in both the print and electronic media, Arnold is a contributing editor of *American Salon* and *Independent Stylist* magazines and a regular columnist for *Independent Stylist*. A member of Toastmasters International, he has appeared on many TV shows, including Oprah Winfrey and the Home Shopping Network, where he features his line of Arnold Zegarelli Products. He also does a monthly beauty and image show on KDKA radio in Pittsburgh.

In his role as a beauty expert and trainer, Arnold has served not only as consultant to many corporations, but as individual mentor and advisor to many of today's leading stylists, a role of which he is particularly proud. For the past 23 years, he has been known for his inspiring lectures and motivational seminars. This book is an outgrowth of his experiences as *someone who listens, someone who knows, and someone who cares.*

Arnold Zegarelli holds a black belt in karate and has boxed as a Golden Gloves finalist. He lives in Pittsburgh with his wife and soul mate, Dolores. They are the parents of two children, Ronda and Gregg.

INDEX OF CONCEPTS

INTRODUCTION

This book is offered as a fountainhead of ideas and strategies for achieving your dreams while acquiring the distinction of being one who not only knows the way and goes the way, but most importantly, shows the way. The target reader is anyone who is thirsty for knowledge.

Diamond Capsules for Success and Wisdom is a collection of 100 gems—Diamond Capsules—that are too illuminating not to be shared with family, friends and co-workers. These Capsules are intended to provide the sparks that can lead to a vibrant light of knowledge and understanding. Their brevity enables rapid and thorough understanding of their concepts.

To assemble these concepts of power, Arnold Zegarelli has spent a lifetime interacting with people from all walks of life, all age groups, backgrounds and lifestyles. It has been said that when the student is ready, the teacher will appear, and because Arnold always strives to be open and receptive, he has had many teachers. One result has been the accumulation of well-thought-out survival principles, gleaned from the trials, tribulations and triumphs of everyday life. He has taken those ideas that have proven most valuable and made them simple and practical—encapsulated them. He now wants to share his knowledge and truths with those who are ready to receive them.

Diamond Capsules are self-contained, blinding glances of insight that are most effective when read a few at a time and fully absorbed. To read these thoughts only once is not enough. This book is designed for continued use and review as situations arise—in short, as a daily inspiration and helpmate for life.

If you are enlightened or inspired by a new concept or two while reading this book, or even if you are reminded convincingly of something you already know, this book will have been a success.

But remember: Knowledge itself is not enough; we must apply what we know.

BALANCED CONCEPTS OF VALUES

There are ten key areas of human values that must be balanced for a full and satisfying life:

Spiritual
Health
    Mental
    Physical
        Nutrition
        Exercise
        Rest
Wealth
Family
Career
Social
Entertainment
Community
Challenges and problems
Golden years: Retirement

The Diamond Capsules that follow are intended to help you know exactly where you are in each of these ten value areas and how to manage them for a richer life.

Diamond Capsules
for Success and Wisdom

KNOW YOURSELF.

*Do an honest evaluation of who you are,
reviewing your strengths,
as well as your weaknesses.*

KNOW HOW YOU GOT TO WHERE YOU ARE.

Learn from your past experiences and memories.
Each event is a lesson.

KNOW WHERE YOU WANT TO GO.

Know what you want to achieve
in each of the ten value areas:
Spiritual, Mental and Physical Health,
Wealth, Family, Career, Social, Entertainment,
Community, Challenges, and Golden Years.
Visualize your desired outcome,
your desired end result, in each area.

BE IN CONTROL
OF YOUR CHOICES
AND THEIR CONSEQUENCES.

Accept responsibility and accountability for your thoughts, words, feelings and actions.

FEELINGS ARE NEITHER RIGHT OR WRONG, THEY JUST ARE.

Respect the other person's right to feel differently;
each person sees the world
from his or her own point of view.

DEVELOP AS MANY REASONS AS POSSIBLE FOR ACHIEVING A SPECIFIC GOAL.

*Your passion and desire are based on
your self-motivation.
If you don't know why, you won't try.
Decide what you want, write it down,
list the reasons, and set a time limit.*

DEVELOP A STRATEGY
AND A PLAN.

Consider your options and choices,
evaluate possible setbacks,
know what you have and what you need.
Also consider who can do what you can't
or don't know how to do.

DO THINGS IN THE PROPER ORDER.

A logical order is fundamental
to achieving a goal.
Think it through.
You don't start a race at the finish line.

HAVE A SELF-IMPROVEMENT PROGRAM BASED ON C.I.P.: THE CONSISTENT INCREMENTAL IMPROVEMENT PROGRAM.

A book is read a page at a time,

a pound is lost or gained an ounce at a time,

and a goal is reached a step at a time.

DEAL WITH LIFE AND RESULTS ON AN "AS IS" BASIS, WHICH IS REALITY.

It does not matter what should or should not be, or what is fair or unfair with life.

It just is.

ACCEPT AND ADJUST
TO EACH SITUATION.
DON'T COMPLAIN OR BLAME;
JUST TRY TO FIND SOME GOOD
OR A LESSON IN IT.

Wishing or hoping that something didn't happen won't change the fact that it did. It is not what happens to you, but what you think, feel and do about it that really matters.

This concept is critical to success, so constantly monitor your attitude and reactions.

WHEREVER YOU ARE, "BE THERE."

Focus on the event.

Stay in the present and enjoy the instant.

That is reality.

AS YOU THINK, SO SHALL YOU FEEL;
AS YOU FEEL, SO SHALL YOU ACT;
AS YOU ACT, SO SHALL OTHERS RESPOND
OR REACT TO YOU.

*You control your world
and your attitude toward it.*

LOOK FOR THE BEST QUALITIES
IN YOURSELF AND OTHERS.

Become a good finder.
What we seek, we usually find,
because we attract to ourselves
only that which we feel worthy of receiving.

FIND YOUR COMPETITIVE EDGE.

Come from your unique strength.
We have all been given gifts from God.
What you do with these gifts is your gift back to Him.

TO HAVE FRIENDS,
YOU MUST FIRST BE A FRIEND.

A friend anticipates your needs;
anticipate those of your friends.

LOOK, SPEAK AND ACT
AS IF YOU ARE THE PERSON
YOU WANT TO BE.

*If you live the role consistently,
you will become that person permanently.*

PRACTICE DISCIPLINE;
IT IS THE CORNERSTONE
OF ALL IMPROVEMENT AND GROWTH.

*Desire, drive and determination
are the wheels, but discipline is their engine.*

MAKE SURE OF THE TRUTH
OF YOUR PREMISES.

If your premises and assumptions are incorrect,
you will be using an incorrect map to get to your destination.
And then, the faster and harder you travel,
the more lost you will become.
Your search for the truth should continue for as long as you do.

VALUE IS THE BONUS
YOU ARE GIVEN
BEYOND THE PRICE PAID.

*When you exceed expectations,
you gain a reputation as someone who performs
even more than you promised.*

YOUR BELIEFS BUILD
YOUR EXPECTATIONS,
AND YOUR EXPECTATIONS
BUILD YOUR OUTCOMES.

Your beliefs about yourself
establish your self-image,
self-confidence and self-esteem.

IF YOU PLANT ROSES,
YOU WILL GET ROSES;
IF YOU PLANT WEEDS,
YOU WILL GET WEEDS.
IF YOU PLANT NOTHING,
YOU WILL STILL GET WEEDS.

Nature punishes inactivity.
Keep planting uplifting thoughts in your mental soil.

WATER AND AIR
ARE ABUNDANT AND FREE.
TO STAY HEALTHY,
TAKE IN AS MUCH AS YOU CAN.

*Fresh, nourishing food is your fuel,
while air and water are the igniters of that fuel.*

WHEN YOU CAN'T SEE
YOUR DESTINATION CLEARLY,
GO AS FAR AS YOU CAN SEE.
FROM THERE, YOU WILL BE ABLE
TO SEE FARTHER.

*After gathering as much information
as you can, take an action. Evaluate feedback, then rest, adjust,
and take an improved action. Continue this process
until the goal or destination has been achieved.*

WHEREVER YOU GO,
YOU TAKE YOURSELF WITH YOU.

*A change of location doesn't necessarily mean
a change in your thinking.
Your thoughts are where you are constantly located.*

WHINING, BLAMING AND COMPLAINING
ARE CALLED "THE REPELLING TRIPLETS,"
BECAUSE OTHERS AVOID PEOPLE
WHO DO THESE TO EXCESS.

Blaming things, such as weather or traffic,

or others, such as employers, co-workers or

groups of people, is a waste of time and energy.

Realize that you cannot control

some things, people, or groups. Accept them and adjust.

Don't blame it, reframe it.

A FAT WALLET MAKES A SOFT PILLOW.

Wealth is what you accumulate beyond your debt.
Your objective in acquiring wealth should be
to enable you to enjoy your chosen retirement lifestyle
on the income earned by that wealth,
without having to withdraw from principal.
You will then indeed be wealthy,
and your capital can remain intact
for you to leave to whomever you choose.

TWO OF THE GREATEST MOTIVATING
FORCES IN THE WORLD ARE
THE SEEKING OF PLEASURE
AND THE AVOIDANCE OF PAIN.

To find out what is perceived as pleasure and pain
in others, you must observe, listen and then
—most important—evaluate a person's behavior.
What they do is more meaningful than what they say.

YOU CANNOT TRULY MOTIVATE OTHERS.
YOU CAN ONLY PRESENT SCENARIOS
AND INCENTIVES, WITH WHICH
THEY MAY MOTIVATE THEMSELVES.

*People generally act
in terms of their own best interests,
responding primarily to "What's in it for me?"
You must understand this
in order to be understood.*

KNOW AND USE A PERSON'S NAME.

*Make the name important to you
by repeating it.
But best of all, associate or link it
with something or someone you already know.*

GIVE SINCERE COMPLIMENTS.

*General compliments such as, "You look wonderful,"
are good. But a specific compliment such as,
"You look wonderful; your skin is glowing," is better.
If you can then widen it with a question, it becomes very special:
"You look wonderful; your skin is glowing. Do you do anything special
to get it that way, or does it just run in your family?"
Tell What you like, Why you like it,
then Widen it with a question, if possible.
This is called the "Three W Compliment."*

TO GATHER MORE INFORMATION,
OR TO KEEP A CONVERSATION BALANCED,
ASK OPEN-ENDED QUESTIONS
THAT CAN'T BE ANSWERED WITH
A SIMPLE "YES" OR "NO".

*Open-ended questions usually begin with
the 5 Ws and an H: Who, What,
Where, When, Why and How.*

DO THE BEST WORK THAT YOU CAN.

You never have to apologize for quality.

CONTROL YOUR TIME,
AND YOU CONTROL
YOUR GREATEST VALUE.

Prioritize your actions.
A's: Must Do; B's: Should Do;
C's: Would Like to Do.
A's are important and pressing.
B's are important but not pressing,
C's are neither pressing nor important.
Spend your time on the important things
before you do the pressing things.

NOBODY CAN RESIST
THE POWER OF BEING PAID
ATTENTION TO.

*One of our greatest human needs is to be recognized,
to feel that we are valuable enough
to be listened to and appreciated.*

THE FEELING BEHIND
GOOD CUSTOMER SERVICE IS,
"MAKE ME FEEL SPECIAL
AND IMPORTANT.
IF YOU DO, I WILL PROBABLY
COME BACK, BUT IF YOU DON'T,
I DEFINITELY WON'T."

*This applies to friends,
as well as to customers and clients.*

WITHOUT PROFIT,
THERE IS EVENTUALLY NO BUSINESS.

Customer satisfaction and profit
are the two requirements of any ongoing business.

TREAT OTHERS THE WAY
THEY WISH TO BE TREATED
NOT THE WAY
YOU WISH TO BE TREATED.

Use this as your new Golden Rule.
"Do unto others as they would have you do unto them."

PUBLIC ACCEPTANCE
AND THE PUBLIC'S DEMAND FOR YOU
WILL DETERMINE
YOUR FINANCIAL SUCCESS.

The public can make or break you.
The public's perception is their reality,
and what they decide affects the entire marketplace.

OUR NON-VERBAL COMMUNICATIONS
SAY A GREAT DEAL ABOUT US.

*Our clothing, accessories, grooming and body language,
such as posture, facial expression, eye contact and gestures,
all send signals about our image.
Image is what people think we are;
identity is what we think we are.*

BALANCE AND MODERATION
IN ALL THINGS IS THE BLEND
THAT BRINGS ABOUT A FULFILLED LIFE.

Too much of any one thing can lead to overkill.

SAY WHAT YOU WANT TO HAPPEN,
NOT WHAT YOU
DON'T WANT TO HAPPEN.

*Say, "Remember to bring home the bread,"
not "Don't forget to bring home the bread."*

TO CORRECT A FAULT IN YOURSELF,
YOU MUST FIRST ADMIT TO HAVING IT.

Denial is the most destructive single obstacle

to behavioral modification and improvement.

Admit and accept; only then can you correct.

THAT WHICH DOES NOT DESTROY YOU,
WILL ONLY MAKE YOU STRONGER
ONCE YOU OVERCOME IT.

*When you are in the midst of a negative situation,
persevere and know that "This, too shall pass."*

PRAISE IN A CROWD;
REPRIMAND IN PRIVATE.

Don't label the person, label the behavior.
For example, say, "You did a selfish thing" instead of,
"You are a selfish person."

ANGER, HATE AND REVENGE
ARE ACIDS THAT DO MORE HARM
TO THE VESSEL THEY ARE STORED IN
THAN TO ANYONE
THEY CAN BE POURED ON.

Why let someone else's behavior control your emotions?

BE A GOOD EXAMPLE.

Show them; don't just tell them.

PROMISE LESS THAN YOU CAN PERFORM, AND THEN PERFORM MORE THAN YOU PROMISED.

*No matter how well you perform,
if it is less than you promised, it is not good enough.*

USE EUPHEMISMS
—BETTER CHOICES OF WORDS
—WHERE APPROPRIATE.

Consider slender, instead of skinny;
economical, instead of cheap;
assertive, instead of pushy;
larger sized, instead of fat.

IT IS NOT JUST WHAT YOU SAY, BUT HOW YOU SAY IT.

Manners, intelligence and verbal skills are the basis of effective communication. Request, don't command or demand.

USE THE "DOUBLE U" CONCEPT FOR CONSISTENT IMPROVEMENT.

Update: Make it newer.

Upgrade: Make it better.

DEVELOP A POSITIVE,
UPBEAT ATTITUDE.

*People are attracted to the charismatic person
who creates an aura of happiness.*

REWARD GOOD BEHAVIOR
AND PERFORMANCE.

*What you compliment, you encourage more of.
Show appreciation and gratitude at every opportunity.*

GIVE ADVICE ONLY WHEN ASKED.

*It is very challenging to refrain from giving suggestions
when you see someone doing something
and you believe you have a better solution or idea.
If it is not your job to critique a person, then don't.*

LOVE WILL MAKE YOU VULNERABLE,
BUT IT ALSO BRINGS YOU
THE GREATEST HAPPINESS.

Love is not a liquid that is depleted as you pour it out.
It is a flame whose warmth is to be shared with others
while it adds light to the world.
When you have learned to love,
you have learned to live.

BEING ABLE TO POSTPONE
INSTANT PLEASURE IS THE FIRST SIGN
OF DISCIPLINE AND MATURITY.

*When you want a great deal in the future,
you have to save it in the present.*

IT'S NOT WHAT YOU GET
IN YOUR QUEST FOR SUCCESS,
IT'S WHAT YOU BECOME
WHILE IN PURSUIT OF IT.

Don't just work to have a million;

work to be worthy of it.

TO HAVE MORE, YOU MUST BE MORE.

*We all want as much as we can get,
but we don't always want to pay the price
in self-development to get it.*

READERS ARE POTENTIAL LEADERS.

The more you read, the more you learn.
The more you learn, the more you can earn.
The more you earn, the more respect
the marketplace will have for you
and the more it will want to follow your example.

TRACK YOUR INCREMENTAL PROGRESS.

Know where you are in relation to
where you want to go.
If you don't keep score, you don't know
whether you are winning or losing in your quest.

WHEN YOU MAKE A MISTAKE,
ADMIT IT QUICKLY AND EMPHATICALLY.

*Tell yourself that it's not like you
to make a mistake like that.
Then tell yourself what you must do
to prevent the mistake from being repeated.*

PEOPLE DON'T CHANGE MUCH
FROM THEIR BASIC NATURES
AND BEHAVIOR PATTERNS.

*Don't assume that you can change people;
it is difficult enough to change ourselves.*

CHANGE CAN BE
EITHER GOOD OR BAD.

Many people assume that change is bad,
just because it represents the unknown
and may force them out of their comfort zones.
But remember that change is inevitable,
so roll with it by accepting and adapting.

KNOWING IS NOT ENOUGH.
WE MUST APPLY WHAT WE KNOW.

We don't become successful for what we know;
we become successful for what we do with what we know.

DEVELOP YOUR VOCABULARY, MANNERS, ETIQUETTE AND CHOICE OF WORDS.

*They are the hallmarks of good self-development.
They oil the cogs in the monotonous grind of everyday life.*

WITHOUT TRUST, THERE IS NO RESPECT;
WITHOUT RESPECT,
THERE IS NO TRUE BONDING.

*Trust cannot be bought
—it must be earned over a period of time
in which promises are kept.*

TRY TO GET ALL THE FACTS
AND NECESSARY INFORMATION
BEFORE MAKING ANY DECISION
OF IMPORTANCE.

To be uninformed is to be unprepared.

COMPROMISE WHEN YOU MUST,
BUT TRY TO MINIMIZE YOUR LOSSES.

When both parties win,
both parties continue to do business.

TO STAY CENTERED
FOR GREATER POWER AND CHARISMA,
BE CONGRUENT WITH YOUR MIND,
BODY AND SOUL.

It is only when you have all three
that you are balanced.

PEOPLE WILL TREAT YOU THE WAY YOU TEACH THEM TO TREAT YOU.

Give people feedback on their behavior,
so they will know your expectations.
If people treat you in an undesirable way
and you don't tell them,
they may assume that you don't mind it,
and they will continue.

YOUR REWARDS
WILL MATCH YOUR SERVICE.

The more service you offer the marketplace,
the more it will pay you.

YOU CANNOT CHANGE NATURE'S LAWS,
SUCH AS GRAVITY, THE TIDES,
THE PASSAGE OF TIME.

Learn them, and use them to your advantage.
Cause and effect is, was, and always will be
the unchangeable principle of nature.

TIME IS THE ESSENCE OF YOUR LIFE.

*Everybody gets 24 hours every day,
and nobody knows how many days they have to live,
so enjoy each day and be thankful for it.*

YOUR VALUE IN THE MARKETPLACE
IS BASED PRIMARILY ON THREE FACTORS.

The demand for your goods and services,
your talent or ability,
and your uniqueness: the difficulty of replacing you.

CONTROL YOUR TEMPER
AND EMOTIONS.

*Being angry punishes you
for someone else's undesirable behavior.
"He who makes me angry, controls me."*

AVOID ARGUMENTS.

Arguing with a fool proves that there are two.

IF YOU CONSTANTLY TAKE FROM SOMEONE
AND NEVER GIVE,
THEY WILL EVENTUALLY RESENT
AND AVOID YOU.

*Ask yourself, "What can I do for the other person?"
You will find an answer if you look for one.*

OCCASIONAL DEFEAT IS UNAVOIDABLE.
LEARN FROM IT.

You are never truly beaten,
no matter how many times you fall.
You are only defeated when you stop trying to get up.

IF YOU TRULY HAVE POWER,
YOU DON'T HAVE TO FLAUNT IT.

*An empty barrel
makes the most noise.*

WHEN YOU EXERCISE,
YOU GIVE YOURSELF A GIFT.

It is better to wear out

than to rust out.

THE BEST WAY
TO GET PEOPLE TO MOTIVATE THEMSELVES
IS TO FIND OUT WHAT THEY LIKE TO DO,
AND GIVE THEM
AN OPPORTUNITY TO DO IT.

Observe, listen and evaluate
what people say and do
to find out what their competitive edge is.

WHEN YOU HUMBLE YOURSELF,
OTHERS WILL EXALT YOU;
BUT WHEN YOU EXALT YOURSELF,
THEY WILL TRY TO HUMBLE YOU.

The reason a thousand mountain streams

pay homage to the sea is

that the sea is beneath them.

OBSTACLES AND ADVERSITY
INTRODUCE YOU TO YOURSELF.

*The captain is tested
on the rough sea.*

PAIN IS THE MIND'S WAY
OF TELLING YOU THAT
SOMETHING IS NOT IN ORDER.

Some pain cannot be eliminated;

it must be endured.

The better your attitude,

the better your tolerance.

LOYALTY IS THE REWARD OF
A MUTUALLY BENEFICIAL RELATIONSHIP.

The best way to ensure loyalty is to be worthy of it.

BOUNCING BACK FROM A SETBACK
IS THE TECHNIQUE THAT
DISCIPLINED MINDS USE
IN THEIR RELENTLESS PURSUIT
OF A GOAL.

*A strong wind can break an oak tree,
but it can only bend a willow branch.*

A SYSTEM IS AN ORGANIZED, CONSISTENT WAY OF DOING THINGS.

*When you are organized,
you can function smoothly with less effort.
First you make your habits,
and then your habits make you.*

STOP MAKING EXCUSES
AND BEGIN TO MAKE PROGRESS.

There are reasons, and there are excuses.
Most people don't want to hear either.
They just want results.

WHEN YOU ARE NOT ACHIEVING
YOUR DESIRED EFFECT,
EXAMINE YOUR BASICS AND PRINCIPLES.

A little learning leads you away from the basics,
but a whole lot of learning brings you back.

GOOD TASTE IS EASIER TO ACQUIRE
WHEN YOU CAN AFFORD AN EXPERT
TO GUIDE YOU.

*Study those who are known to have good taste
and do likewise.*

FEAR IS A DARKROOM
WHERE ONLY NEGATIVES DEVELOP.

The acronym for fear is
False Evidence Appearing Real.
When we are afraid,
we actually become more vulnerable.

HAPPINESS IS SOMETIMES
JUST HAVING SOMETHING PLEASANT
AND POSITIVE TO LOOK FORWARD TO.

Plan an experience that will reward you

for your present efforts.

INJURIES OCCASIONALLY
HAPPEN TO EVERYONE.

Don't ask, "Why Me?"
or "Why Now?"
Just accept the situation,
and do what you have to do
to heal quickly and properly.

VISUALIZE WHAT YOU WANT TO ACHIEVE, NOT WHAT YOU WANT TO AVOID.

We don't always get what we want,
but we can almost always get what we visualize.
We are all creative
when we set the child within us free to soar.

PATIENCE IS A VIRTUE
THAT WISE PEOPLE HAVE,
INTELLIGENT PEOPLE WANT,
AND IMPULSIVE PEOPLE NEED TO LEARN.

Patience is to see grass, but think milk.

WHEN YOU ARE STUCK,
OR WHEN YOU REACH A PLATEAU
IN YOUR QUEST TOWARD A GOAL,
REASSESS YOUR SITUATION.

That is when you must replenish your desire

to trigger your determination and drive.

DON'T COMPARE YOURSELF TO OTHERS.

*If they are weak you will believe you are strong,
and if they are strong you will think you are weak.
Work toward your own potential,
regardless of those around you.*

WORK AND SAVE
WHILE YOU ARE YOUNG,
SO YOU CAN REST
IN YOUR LATER YEARS.

*Some people do just the opposite.
They wonder why they are dependent on the government
or others during what should be their golden years.*

BEING EFFICIENT
IS DOING THINGS RIGHT,
BUT BEING EFFECTIVE
IS DOING THE RIGHT THINGS.

Don't mistake activity for progress.

Activity is movement,

but progress is movement

directed to a desired outcome.

SUCCESSFUL PEOPLE
BECOME SUCCESSFUL BECAUSE
THEY DO THE THINGS THAT
UNSUCCESSFUL PEOPLE CAN'T
OR WON'T DO.

*Take action on your dreams,
or they will remain just dreams.*

SUCCESS

True success cannot be measured by your financial or social status, the number of diplomas bearing your name or whether or not you are a famous celebrity. Success is a state of mind. It is a reflection of your heart.

Each of us is responsible for our own success. We must follow our hearts. By keeping our vision at the forefront of our lives, we will naturally follow the path to our own personal success. Sometimes that path is rocky, and we may even take a detour, but sheer determination and tenacity will pay off. Setting our sights on realistic, predetermined goals can help us stay on track.

On some days, our measure of success may simply be that we have survived the day. Nonetheless, that alone can be a monumental task worthy of recognition! Each small step brings us closer to our specific goals. I hope that this book has aided you on your journey toward those goals.

Don't be afraid to aim high. It is better to aim at a star than to shoot down a well; you are bound to hit a higher mark.

BONUS GEMS

FIVE LAWS OF POSITIVE ACHIEVING

1ST LAW:

Decide on what you want to achieve. Vividly imagine it.

Believe and know that it is possible.

Write it down. Be specific.

Know where you are in relation to your desired outcome.

Set a time limit.

Make a decision to do it and begin with the outcome clearly visualized.

2ND LAW:

Take the responsibility for making it happen.

3RD LAW:

Strategy: Know and plan the steps to take, and do things
in their proper logical order.

4TH LAW:

Evaluate feedback.

Follow a consistent incremental improvement program.

Deal positively with plateaus, challenges, problems and setbacks.

Track and record your progress.

Continue relentlessly, while adapting to new information and circumstances.

5TH LAW:

Enjoy the quest.

L.A.T.I.P.A.C. FOR SUCCESS
SEVEN KEYS

Love
Attitude
Talent
Image
Purpose
Action
Communication

L.A.T.I.P.A.C. is *CAPITAL* spelled backwards!

THE NOBLE QUARTET
NEEDED FOR
MEANINGFUL RELATIONSHIPS

Trust
Respect
Common Goals
Bonding

Copies of this book may be ordered from
          Zegarelli, Inc.
          177 Shadow Ridge Drive
          Pittsburgh PA 15238
          Telephone 412-967-9288

For single copies, please send check or money order for $12.95 plus $2.00 for shipping and handling. Bulk copies for premiums, promotions, fund-raising or educational purposes may be ordered at discount. Contact the Special Sales Director at the address above.